WE BUILT THIS CITY

BOSTON

Tamra B. Orr

PURPLE TOAD
PUBLISHING

Purple Toad
PUBLISHING

Printing   1   2   3   4   5   6   7   8   9

WE BUILT THIS CITY

BOSTON

CHICAGO

LOS ANGELES

NEW YORK

PHILADELPHIA

Library of Congress Cataloging-in-Publication Data
Orr, Tamara, B.
   We Built this City: Boston / Written by Tamara B. Orr.
      p. cm.
Includes bibliographic references, glossary, and index.
ISBN 9781624694127
1. United States Local History–Boston–Juvenile Literature. 2. Cities–Urban–Geography–Juvenile Literature. I. Series: We Built this City: Boston.
 F73.5.A45GF125 2019
 974.46
                                        Library of Congress Control Number: 2018943937
eBook ISBN: 9781624694110

ABOUT THE AUTHOR: Tamra B. Orr is a full-time author who lives in the Pacific Northwest. She has written more than 500 educational books for readers of all ages. A graduate of Ball State University in Muncie, Indiana, Orr is the mother of four and a lifetime letter writer. In addition, she loves to hop in the car for long road trips, and heading east to Boston is high on her list of adventures.

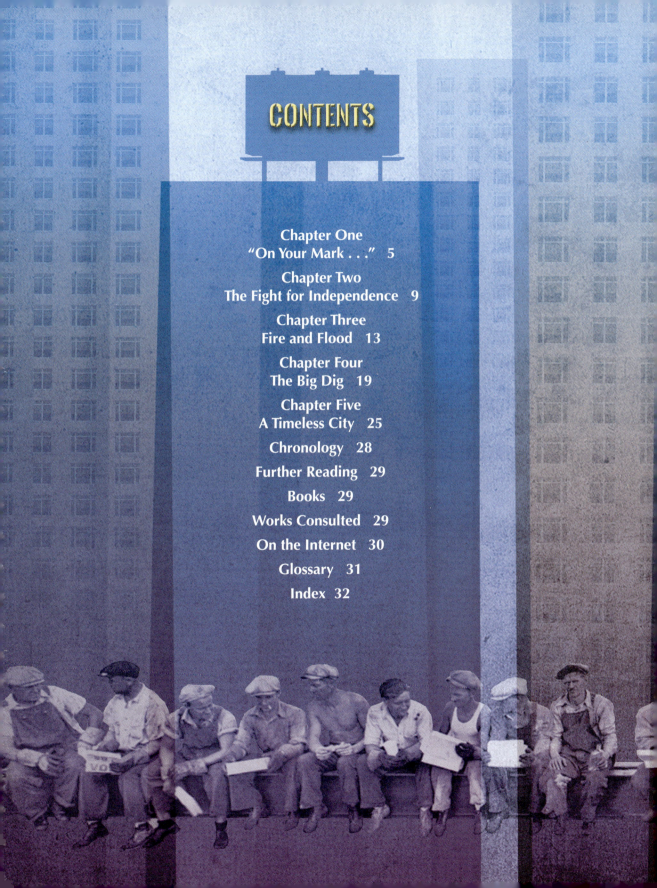

CONTENTS

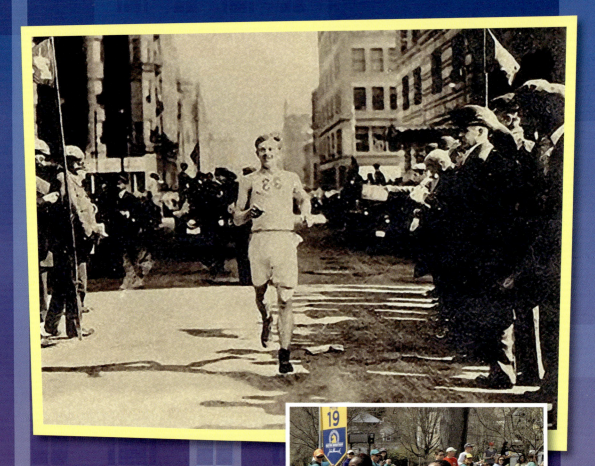

Above: Fred S. Cameron wins the Boston Marathon in 1910. Right: In 2016, runners make the same trip.

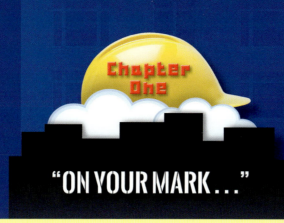

"ON YOUR MARK..."

At just after noon on a spring day in April 1897, fifteen men stood at the starting line. They tried hard to be patient. Most had arrived in Boston early that morning by train and had been waiting for hours. Now they stretched, working to warm up and loosen their muscles as the crowd around them grew restless. Everyone was waiting for the event to begin. No one there could have had any idea that they were about to start a Boston tradition that would last more than a century.

At last, at 12:19 p.m., the starter said the golden word: "Go!" The men all surged forward. The first Boston Marathon had begun.

One of the men who had helped organize the U.S. marathon team for the Olympics, John Graham, along with local businessman Herbert Holton, had brought the race to Boston. They decided to hold it on Patriot's Day. This holiday, celebrated in Massachusetts and Maine, honors the start of the Revolutionary War.

As the minutes and the miles passed, the runners focused on pacing themselves. The 24.5-mile route ran from Metcalf's Mill in Ashland to Boston's Irving Street Oval near Copley Square. It had uneven ground, curves, and hills. As the men ran, they had constant company. Soldiers rode bicycles alongside each man, ready to hand out water, lemons, or wet handkerchiefs. They were also there to help anyone who got hurt—or gave up before the finish line.

The hardest part of the run was, without question, Heartbreak Hill. Whether the runner was in first place, last place, or somewhere in the

John J. McDermott was the first winner of the Boston Marathon. He ran again in 1898 and came in fourth.

middle, he cringed when reaching it. Located between miles 20 and 21, it was not terribly high. It was only about 91 feet. But it had a very steep rise. By the time the runners reached it, they were usually quite tired. Gearing up to tackle the hill was daunting.

The hill got its name during the 1936 marathon. As the story goes, runner Johnny Kelley passed his top rival, Tarzan Brown. As he ran by, he patted him on the back. Brown was so upset he powered through and won the race. When a *Boston Globe* reporter wrote about the moment in the newspaper, he stated that losing "broke Kelley's heart." A nickname was born— "Heartbreak Hill"—and it stuck..

New Yorker John J. McDermott won the first Boston marathon. Since then, it has been held every year for more than a century. Of course, there have been many changes since that day in 1897. In 1924, the course was lengthened to 26.2 miles. While only 15 men participated in the first race, today the event attracts more than 30,000 men and women. In the 2017 Boston Marathon, just under half of the 27,222 runners were women. In 1975, a wheelchair division was added to the race. In 2017, there were 53 participants in this division, and everyone completed the course. About half a million people come to Boston to watch the race each year.

During the 2013 Marathon, there was a terrorist bombing. Three people were killed. More than 300 were injured. Instead of scaring people away from the event, however, the following year the race had more participants than ever. Today, the Boston Marathon is watched worldwide. Thousands of tourists come to the city to see what they can in person. While there, they take the time to explore the city and its rich history, breathtaking sites, and delicious seafood. Welcome to Boston!

Every year, tourists and locals watch Boston Marathon runners wind through the city.

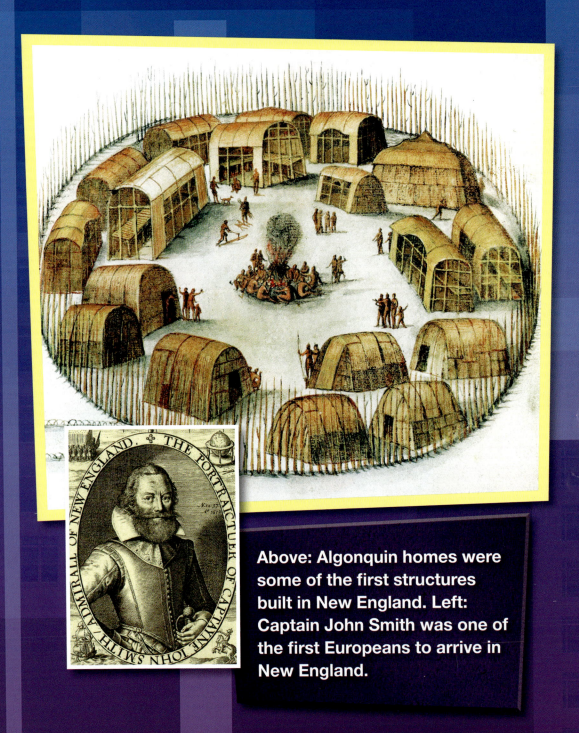

Above: Algonquin homes were some of the first structures built in New England. Left: Captain John Smith was one of the first Europeans to arrive in New England.

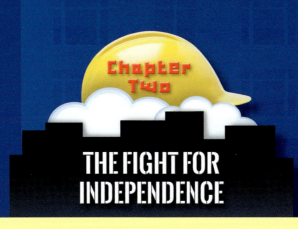

Chapter Two

THE FIGHT FOR INDEPENDENCE

The first people to live in the area of the future Boston were Native Americans. In 2400 BCE, most lived on a peninsula called Shawnut. The name means "land of many waters." The peninsula was made up of rolling hills, including Mount Vernon, Beacon Hill, and Pemberton Hill. One day settlers would refer to these three as the Trimount. By 1600 CE, more than 100,000 Algonquin lived throughout what would one day be New England.

In the early seventeenth century, some of the first Europeans sailed down the coast of these lands. Soldier and explorer Captain John Smith led the expedition. For more than two years, Smith mapped the northeast coast. To make it sound more inviting to possible colonists, the British captain called the region New England. He named the southern river Charles, in honor of England's Prince Charles. The northern one was called Kennebec River. This river was named for the bay it flows into. In the Abenaki language, *Kennebec* means "bay."

As more Europeans came to explore this area, they brought along new types of food and weapons—and new illnesses. In 1617, a smallpox epidemic came ashore with these explorers. Within a year, three-quarters of the Native Americans had died. More epidemics swept through in 1690, 1702, and 1721, killing hundreds.

In England, religious laws were very strict. Some groups wanted to leave and start new churches in the New World. In 1620, the *Mayflower* brought 102 pilgrims to the shores of what would be

After Blackstone moved from this house on Beacon Hill, 50 acres of his land became Boston Common.

Massachusetts. In 1623, another explorer arrived. The Reverend William Blaxton (or Blackstone) also wanted to set up a religious settlement. To his surprise, the land he and the others had planned to live on was already occupied.

Although most of the other travelers returned to England, Blaxton remained. He built a cabin and planted an orchard on 800 acres on the western slope of the future Beacon Hill. The Reverend became the Boston area's first permanent European resident.

Within a few years, Puritans and Quakers immigrated to the area. From that point on, the region grew quickly. By 1630, the city of Boston had already formed. It had its first official governor. By the end of the 1600s, it had its first school, a mint that produced the country's first paper money, a newspaper, and a printing press.

A Time of War

The second half of the eighteenth century was full of conflict and fighting for Boston. The Thirteen Colonies remained under England's control. That is not what they wanted. They had left Europe to find religious freedom, as well as a chance to start new lives. They wanted their own nation: the United States. England was not about to let them go that easily, however.

On March 10, 1765, Britain passed the Stamp Act. It placed a tax on all kinds of papers—from newspapers and legal documents to licenses and playing cards. Colonists were not happy. They had to pay the tax, but they had no say in how the money was used. This was known as "taxation without representation." Inspired, people from nine

The Old State House remains one of the oldest public buildings in the United States.

of the colonies sat down and wrote a Declaration of Rights and presented it to the British. They demanded the Stamp Act be repealed. It finally was—but not until March 18, 1766. The people of Boston celebrated by decorating their homes, shooting off fireworks, and ringing bells throughout the city.

England was not finished with the colonies. In 1768, it sent troops to Boston to remind them that the British were still in control. Tensions increased and erupted on March 5, 1770. A fight broke out in front of Boston's Old State House. A group of people began hurling insults—and snowballs—at a "redcoat," or British soldier. Stones replaced the snowballs. Then clubs came out. The soldier ran for help. When the fighting was over, five civilians were dead. Colonists called the melee the Boston Massacre.

It was not long before the British and the colonists were fully engaged in battle, led by General George Washington. On April 19, 1775, the Revolutionary War officially began. British troops faced local soldiers at Lexington and Concord, near Boston. On July 4, 1776, the colonists declared their independence from Britain. The war lasted for eight years. Finally, the British surrendered, and the Treaty of Paris officially freed the colonies in September 1783.

By this time, Boston was one of the largest cities in the United States. It had a population of about 15,000—and they were now officially Americans.

The Boston and Lowell Railroad Station was one of the first in the United States. Inset: A replica of a Planet-class steam locomotive from around 1830. Early locomotives often jumped the tracks.

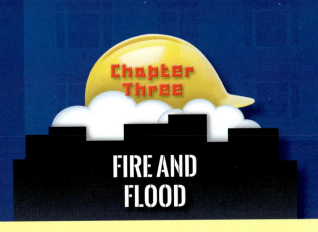

FIRE AND FLOOD

The Boston of the mid to late 1800s was thriving and crowded. Close to 100,000 people were living there. More and more homes and businesses were built. Miles of railroad track were laid to move people at the roaring speed of 20 miles per hour.

On the evening of November 9, 1872, in the basement of a dry goods warehouse, a small fire started. Soon, flames engulfed the building and spread. Although many buildings were made of stone and brick, they had wooden window frames, trim, and roofs. The wood, combined with the narrowness of the streets, allowed the fire to race down the streets. It burned uncontrolled for 12 straight hours.

The fire department faced many challenges. The city's water mains were old. They had not been upgraded to deal with the city's growing population. Water supplies were limited. The fire trucks were pulled by horses. In a case of bad timing, most of the city's horses were ill, making them slow and clumsy. The Boston firefighters desperately telegraphed neighboring cities for help. However, because it was late, most telegraph offices were already closed.

The Great Boston Fire destroyed 65 acres of property. It burned down 776 buildings and did billions of dollars' worth of damage (in 2018 money values). More than a dozen people died. The fire did more than that, however. It changed how the city was built.

Rebuilding Boston happened almost immediately. Strict building codes and fire laws were put into place to keep the city safer and more fireproof. Regular fire inspections were required. The downtown area most damaged by the fire originally held rows of warehouses, small businesses, and elegant mansions. This all changed with the rebuilding.

A number of larger businesses saw this burned land as the perfect chance to expand into downtown. Many built new offices there. They were creating Boston's first financial district.

Today, Boston's financial district is a fascinating mix of old and new. It is often considered the heart of all of New England's banking and finance. The city's first skyscraper, the Boston Custom House Tower, was built from 1913 to 1915. Its foundation is from the original 1849 custom house. While the financial district has the historically famous Old South Meeting House and the Bell-in-Hand Tavern, both built in the mid-1700s, it also has sparkling skyscrapers, banks, condos, and stores.

Standing at 496 feet tall, the Custom House Tower has columns carved from a single piece of granite from nearby Quincy. The building is supported by 3,000 wood piles driven down to the bedrock.

In 1919, a flood of molasses destroyed buildings and claimed 21 lives.

A Ferocious Flood

On a mild January afternoon in 1919, Boston's North End was bustling. The city was full of sounds: the clopping of horses' hooves, the rumble of the elevated train, and the hum of countless conversations. In the background, the nearby Purity Distilling Company's huge metal tank groaned and moaned. No one paid any attention to it. The tank had been making those sounds ever since it had been built four years earlier. At 50 feet tall and 90 feet in diameter, the tank held 2.3 million gallons of molasses. It was to be used for making alcohol for rum and in ammunition. The tank had been built quickly. A number of safety features were overlooked.

Suddenly, the air was filled with a terrifying metallic screech. The half-inch-thick metal rivets holding the Purity Distilling Company's tank together gave way. They flew through the air like shrapnel. As the sides

The Boston Daily Globe EXTRA

MOLASSES TANK EXPLOSION INJURES 50 AND KILLS 11

For a long time after the Molasses Flood, it was the only thing the newspapers talked about.

of the tank tore open, one witness stated, "It was like someone was on the inside hammering to get out." A 15-foot-tall wave of molasses moving at 35 miles per hour swept over the North End. The elevated train was pulled off its tracks as its solid steel supports snapped. Buildings toppled or were pushed off their foundations. An article in *The Boston Globe* stated the buildings "cringed up as though they were made of pasteboard." People were knocked off their feet and covered in a two- to three-foot layer of molasses.

Help arrived immediately. Police officers, firefighters, and more than one hundred sailors from the USS *Nantucket* rushed to pull people and animals out of the muck. They had to move quickly. Cooling temperatures would harden the molasses.

Cleanup took weeks as mere soap and water was not enough to cut through the molasses. Instead, workers used saltwater from the nearby Atlantic Ocean.

The Great Molasses Flood killed 21 people. More than 150 were injured. The Purity Distilling Company was found at fault for not meeting safety standards when the tank was built. The steel plates on the tank were too thin to support the heavy molasses. Not enough rivets were used. Because of this disaster, Boston's businesses were held to stricter safety codes and regular inspections.

Today, the site of the flood is a playground and a baseball field. Ask some of the people who live close by. They will tell you, on hot summer nights, the sweet scent of molasses is still carried on the breeze.

1. **Purity Distilling molasses tank**
2. **Firehouse 31 (heavy damage)**
3. **Paving department and police station**
4. **Purity offices (flattened)**
5. **Copp's Hill Terrace**
6. **Boston Gas Light Building (damaged)**
7. **Purity warehouse (mostly intact)**
8. **Residential area (where houses were flattened)**

Starting in the 1820s, Irish, Italian, and many other immigrants came to Boston to live and work to build the city. Immigrant Donald McKay created a shipyard in 1845 (right) and for over 40 years produced ships that broke speed records.

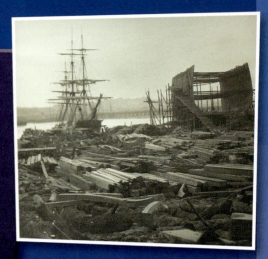

Irish immigrant Charles E. Logue designed Boston's immortal Fenway Park. The park is home to the "Green Monster"—a 37-foot-tall wooden wall.

THE BIG DIG

It seemed like a good idea at the time.

As Boston grew, so did the city's traffic jams. By the late 1940s, it was clear that something needed to be done to streamline the long rows of traffic. In 1948, the city began building a six-lane elevated highway. It reached from Boston's downtown to its waterfront. In order to construct the highway, 1,000 buildings had to be torn down. More than 20,000 Bostonians had to move.

The construction was finished in 1959. The highway was designed to handle about 75,000 vehicles every single day—which it did. However, by the 1990s, more than 190,000 vehicles were crossing it—or attempting to. The traffic was terrible. It tended to be bumper to bumper for up to 16 hours a day. The accident rate was four times the national average. Experts began predicting the highway was going to fail structurally at any moment. By the 1980s, city planners were discussing replacing it. The project seemed too daunting.

For several years, city planners and architects tried to figure out how to replace the elevated highway without having to shut it down in the process. How could people continue to drive through the city while an entirely new system was being built right near it? At first, the city considered building a system of suspension bridges. In the end, they decided to go the opposite direction—they would build underground tunnels with expressways 8 to 14 lanes wide. At least this way, no one would be pushed out of their homes to make way for bulldozers.

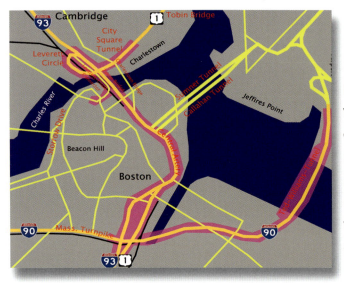

Plans for the Big Dig (in pink) resulted in this new route with bridges and tunnels under or near existing highways.

While the official name for the new project was the Central Artery, it quickly earned the nickname of the Big Dig. A reporter for the *Boston Globe* said that the project was "a moonshot-caliber engineering challenge." Construction began in 1993. Soon, the city realized just how difficult a goal it had set.

More than 16 million cubic yards of dirt had to be dug out. That was enough to fill a sports stadium all the way to the top—16 times! It required 541,000 truckloads to move away all that dirt. About two-thirds of the dirt was taken to area landfills. More than 4,400 loads were sent by barge to Spectacle Island in Boston Harbor. A new park was built on it. The project used so much reinforced steel that it could have wrapped around the entire planet at the equator.

The Zakim Bridge is made of steel and concrete.

Building highway I-93 underground cut down on noise and air pollution in the city.

The digging was underneath the old highway, which was still being used. The underground highways required more than 3.8 million cubic yards of concrete. That is enough to create a sidewalk, three feet wide and four inches thick, from Boston to San Francisco and back—three times. The project's scope was so large that experts compared it to creating the Panama Canal or England's Chunnel. More than 5,000 people worked on it.

The city promised not to bother people during the construction. Utilities were not to be disturbed. Since people living in nearby apartments could not keep their windows open during the summer because of the noise, the city paid for their air conditioning and soundproof windows. Some people even got free firm mattresses to counteract the shaking from the nearby earthmoving equipment.

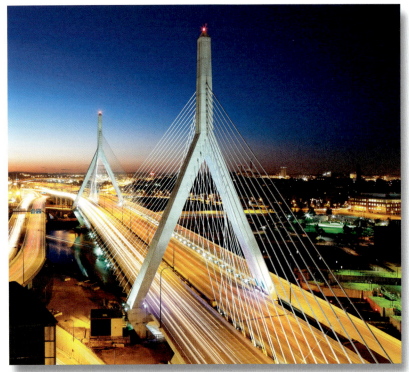

The cable-stayed Zakim Bridge carries ten lanes of traffic across the Charles River. It connects Cambridge and Boston.

The Central Artery was finished in 2003. It had soared past the predicted cost of $2.6 billion to $15 billion. This made it one of the most expensive construction projects in U.S. history. It took eight more years than planned to finish, thanks to a series of unexpected events. Blueprints did not line up properly. Concrete was mixed improperly. When used, it leaked. At one point, ceilings collapsed. Then, near the South Station rail yards, the soil was so unstable, workers could not stand on it to work. To solve the problem, refrigerator units were brought in. They were used to freeze the ground so that work could continue.

All the effort, time, and money had a huge impact. Commuting time was cut in half with the new expressways. Because traffic keeps moving, there are fewer emissions, so there is less air pollution. Boston's carbon monoxide levels dropped 12 percent once the Central Artery opened.

The new expressways could easily handle more than the 536,000 vehicles that use them daily. The Big Dig brought many tourists to the city. This extra tourism improved the city's economy. In addition to the expressways, the city created more than 45 parks and public plazas where the elevated highways once ran. Instead of traffic jams, the area now has hundreds of trees and countless happy visitors.

Boston Symphony Hall began construction in 1889. The architects hired a Harvard physicist, Wallace Clement Sabine, to help with the shape of the walls, the placement of the seats, the angles for the stage, and the use of materials like felt to help produce the best sound. It has remained a treasure for Boston's music scene. The stage floor was restored in 2006 using the same maple wood and style of nails used in 1889.

Boston embraces the old while continuing to grow. Top: The Museum of Fine Arts hosts over one million visitors a year. Middle: Founded in 1634, Boston Common is America's oldest public park. Bottom: The 60-story Millennium Tower Boston was completed in 2016. It holds over 420 luxury homes.

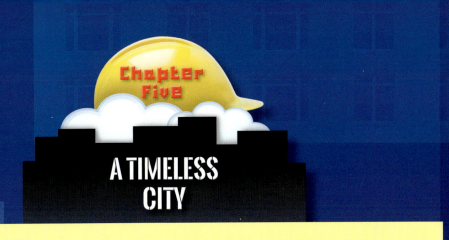

A TIMELESS CITY

Boston reflects the rich history of the past and the shining potential of the future. Memorials, plaques, statues, and historic buildings and sites are scattered throughout the city that once was the center for the fight for the country's independence.

One of Boston's most popular tourist attractions is the Freedom Trail. The tour winds for 2.5 miles through the city. It begins at Boston Common. This is where the first militia from the colonies trained to fight. It is also where British troops camped before heading to the battle of Concord at the start of the Revolutionary War. Another stop is the Old Granary Burial Grounds. Many patriots and war heroes are buried there, including Paul Revere and Samuel Adams. Tourists often spend extra time at the Old State House. This is where Bostonians gathered on July 18, 1776, to hear the Declaration of Independence read aloud. Still others enjoy walking through Paul Revere's house. It is made of carved timber and fastened by wooden pegs. Every stop on the Freedom Trail is a glimpse into America's past.

Boston honors its past, but it is also focused on its future. In July 2017, the city published a huge report called "Imagine Boston 2030." Based on the input of more than 15,000 experts and residents, this plan describes how the city will change over the next few decades.

Boston's population is only going to grow in the coming years. In 2017, its population was 656,000. Experts predicted it would reach 724,000 by 2030 and 800,000 by 2050. The city planned to build thousands more apartments, homes, and condos. It would also need

At 790 feet high, the John Hancock Tower is the tallest building in Boston. People on the upper floors used to get motion sickness when the building swayed in the wind. A tuned-mass damper (inset), which reduces vibrations, was installed on the 58th floor to help stabilize the building.

hotels, restaurants, supermarkets, shops, and offices. Many of these homes and businesses would be housed in soaring skyscrapers.

Boston also planned to make the city more "green," or eco-friendly. It would create more open spaces and use fewer fossil fuels. The plan also called for more flood protection at the waterfront. This would provide safety from the rising water levels predicted to occur because of climate change.

The Franklin Park Zoo is part of the Emerald Necklace, which is a 1,100-acre chain of parks that winds through Boston and Brooklyn.

Whether walking through Boston in order to experience a taste of the past or strolling through to see how the future might change this great city, visitors are sure to be amazed. The city is a continuing work in progress. It reaches for new possibilities while standing on the shoulders of some of the nation's most important moments in history.

Boston can claim a lot of firsts, including the first chocolate factory in the U.S.

27

CHRONOLOGY

BCE

2400 Native Americans are living on Shawmut.

1600 More than 100,000 Algonquin live throughout the area that will one day be called New England.

CE

1614 Captain John Smith explores the coast of what he calls New England.

1617 Europeans bring the disease smallpox to New England. It devastates the Native American population there, taking three of every four lives.

1620 The *Mayflower* brings 102 passengers from England to Massachusetts. These pilgrims want to start a new church in the New World.

1623 The Reverend William Blaxton (or Blackstone) arrives from England to set up a religious settlement. He settles on Beacon Hill.

1630 Boston is officially a city.

1765 The British pass the Stamp Act, which taxes colonists for using paper. The tax is repealed the following March.

1770 During the Boston Massacre, Boston patriots taunt British troops, who fire back at the crowd. Five civilians are killed.

1775 The Revolutionary War begins on April 19 at the Battle of Concord, near Boston.

1776 Delegates from the Thirteen Colonies sign the Declaration of Independence. On July 18, Bostonians gather at the Old State House to hear the document read aloud.

1783 The British surrender, and the Treaty of Paris ends the Revolutionary War.

1872 A fire razes hundreds of buildings in downtown Boston. The city will rebuild using stricter building codes and fire laws.

1897 The first Boston Marathon is run in April.

1915 The city's first skyscraper, the Boston Custom House Tower, is completed.

1919 In January, a huge tank holding 2.3 million gallons of molasses bursts, sending a 15-foot-tall wave of sticky goo through an Italian-American neighborhood. The Great Molasses Flood will cover several city blocks and claim the lives of 21 people.

1948 Boston begins building an elevated highway designed to relieve traffic jams. It will be completed in 1959.

1993 Work on the Big Dig begins.

2003   The Central Artery is completed. Its total cost is $15 billion.

2013   Terrorists bomb the Boston Marathon. Three people die and more than 300 are injured.

2017   A report called "Imagine Boston 2030" outlines plans for how Boston will grow over the next few decades.

FURTHER READING

Books

Baby Professor. *What Happened at the Boston Massacre?* Newark, DE: Baby Professor Books, 2017.

Petersen, Justin. *Boston Marathon (World's Greatest Sporting Events)*. Oakland, CA: Scobre Educational, 2015.

Shea, Therese. *The Boston Massacre (What You Didn't Know about History)*. New York: Gareth Stevens, 2014.

Winters, Kay. *Colonial Voices: Hear Them Speak: The Outbreak of the Boston Tea Party Told from Multiple Points of View*. New York: Puffin Books, 2015.

Yee, Kristina, and Frances Poletti. *The Girl Who Ran: Bobbi Gibb, The First Woman to Run the Boston Marathon*. Seattle, WA: Compendium Inc., 2017.

Works Consulted

Acitelli, Tom. "12 Boston Developments Set to Transform the City." *Boston Curbed*. May 14, 2017. https://boston.curbed.com/maps/boston-developments-new-2017

Andres, Evan. "The Great Molasses Flood of 1919." History.com. January 13, 2017. http://www.history.com/news/the-great-molasses-flood-of-1919

Brooke, Rebecca Beatrice. History of Massachusetts. http://historyofmassachusetts.org ©2018

Enwemeka, Zeninjor. "Plan Provides Road Map for What Boston Should Look Like in 2030." *WBUR*. July 11, 2017. http://www.wbur.org/bostonomix/2017/07/11/imagine-boston-2030-final-plan

FURTHER READING

Flint, Anthony. "10 Years Later, Did the Big Dig Deliver?" *The Boston Globe*, December 29, 2015. https://www.bostonglobe.com/magazine/2015/12/29/years-later-did-big-dig-deliver/tSb8PIMS4QJUETsMpA7Spl/story.html

Gelinas, Nicole. "Lessons of Boston's Big Dig." *City Journal*. Autumn 2007. https://www.city-journal.org/html/lessons-boston%E2%80%99s-big-dig-13049.html

"Globe Coverage of the First Boston Marathon." Boston.com. April 20, 1897, http://archive.boston.com/marathon/history/1897_globe.htm

Herwick, Edgar. "From 'Beantown' to 'The Hub,' How Did Boston Earn Its Nicknames?" *WGBH News*, August 30, 2017. https://news.wgbh.org/2017/08/30/local-news/beantown-hub-how-did-boston-earn-its-nicknames

Mancini, Mark. "Why Is Boston Called 'Beantown'?" *Mental Floss*. May 16, 2014. http://mentalfloss.com/article/56690/why-boston-called-beantown

Massachusetts Department of Transportation. "The Big Dig." Undated. http://www.massdot.state.ma.us/highway/TheBigDig/ProjectBackground.aspx

"Recap of the First Boston Marathon (1897)." *Click Americana*. Undated. https://clickamericana.com/media/newspapers/recap-of-the-first-boston-marathon-1897

Stanly, Robert. "The Great Molasses Flood." *New England Today*. January 15, 2018. https://newengland.com/today/living/new-england-history/great-molasses-flood/

On the Internet

Boston Athletic Association's The Boston Marathon: Bring the Kids
http://www.baa.org/races/10k/event-information/bring-the-kids.aspx

Ducksters: The Boston Tea Party
http://www.ducksters.com/history/boston_tea_party.php

Ducksters: Massachusetts State History
http://www.ducksters.com/geography/us_states/massachusetts_history.php

Social Studies for Kids: Boston Marathon Winners
http://www.socialstudiesforkids.com/articles/sports/bostonmarathon-famous.htm

GLOSSARY

Abenaki (ah-beh-NAH-kee)—A member of a group of Native Americans who lived in northern New England; the language of the Abenaki.

ammunition (am-yoo-NIH-shun)—Explosive materials used as weapons.

carbon monoxide (KAR-bin muh-NOK-syd)—A colorless, odorless gas that contributes to air pollution.

civilian (sih-VIL-yin)—A person who is not in the military.

colonist (KAH-luh-nist)—A person who lives in a colony, which is any area outside the country that governs it.

commute (kuh-MYOOT)—To travel on a regular route to and from work.

eco-friendly (EE-koh FREND-lee)—Not harmful to the environment.

economy (ee-KAH-nuh-mee)—The exchange of goods and services in a community.

emissions (ee-MIH-shuns)—Energy or materials released after a chemical process.

epidemic (eh-pih-DEH-mik)—Widespread; affecting many people.

expedition (ek-speh-DIH-shun)—An organized trip.

fossil fuels (FAH-sul fyoolz)—Materials such as coal, gas, and oil that are mined from the earth and burned for energy.

grueling (GROO-ling)—Extremely difficult and tiring.

massacre (MAS-ih-kur)—The deliberate killing of many people.

melee (MEH-lay)—A confused fight.

mint (MINT)—A place that prints or molds currency (money).

mitigation (mih-tih-GAY-shun)—The process of making something less severe or damaging.

pasteboard (PAYST-bord)—Thick cardboard.

peninsula (peh-NIN-soo-luh)—A piece of land that projects into water.

repeal (ree-PEEL)—To undo (a law).

rivet (RIH-vet)—A short metal fastener with a head on each end.

smallpox (SMALL-poks)—A deadly disease that infects the skin.

INDEX